Merry

CHRISTMAS

This Books Belongs To

....

....

....

....

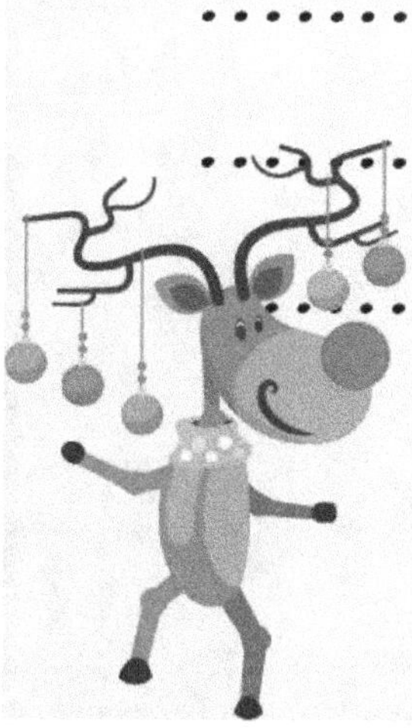

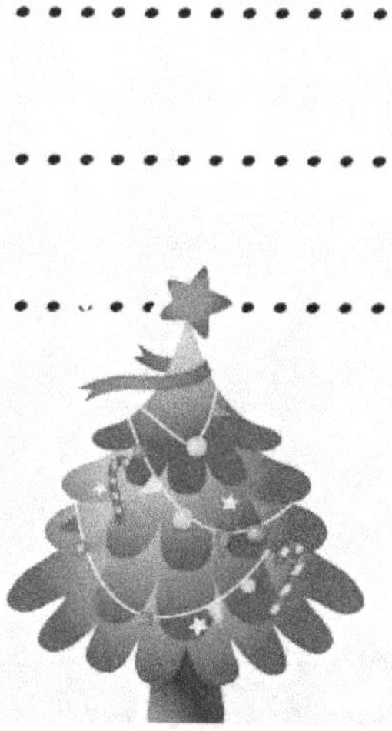

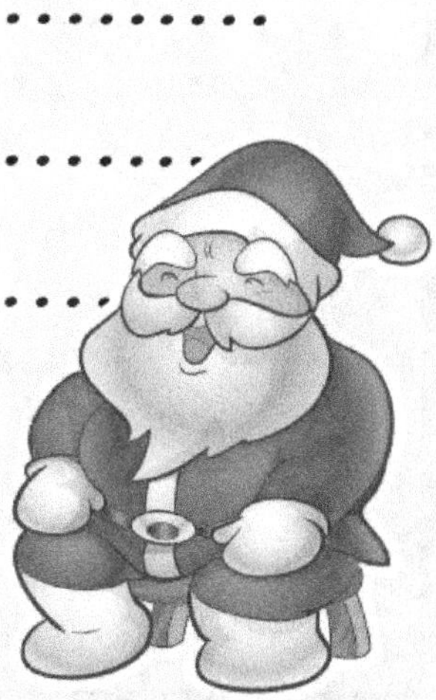

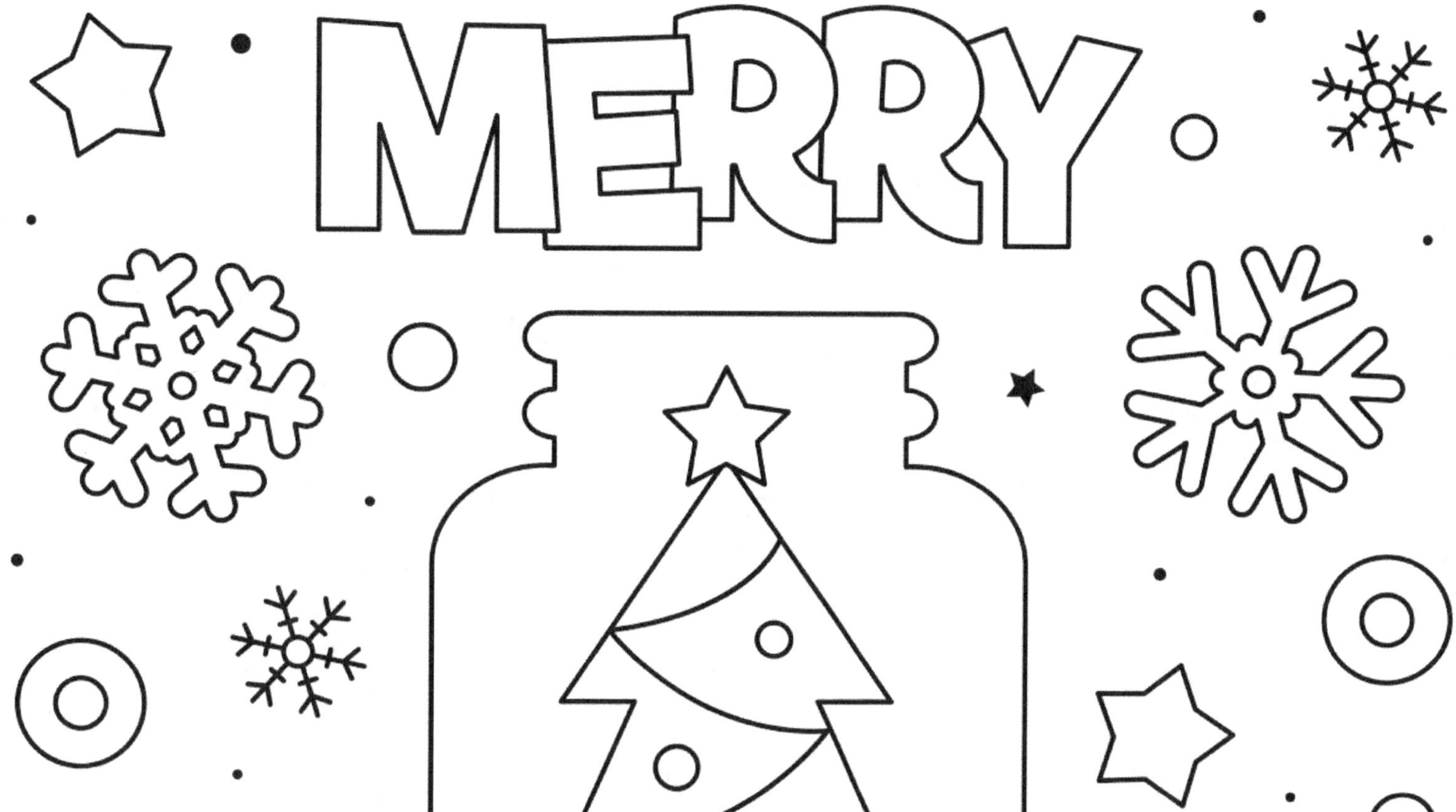
MERRY
CHRISTMAS

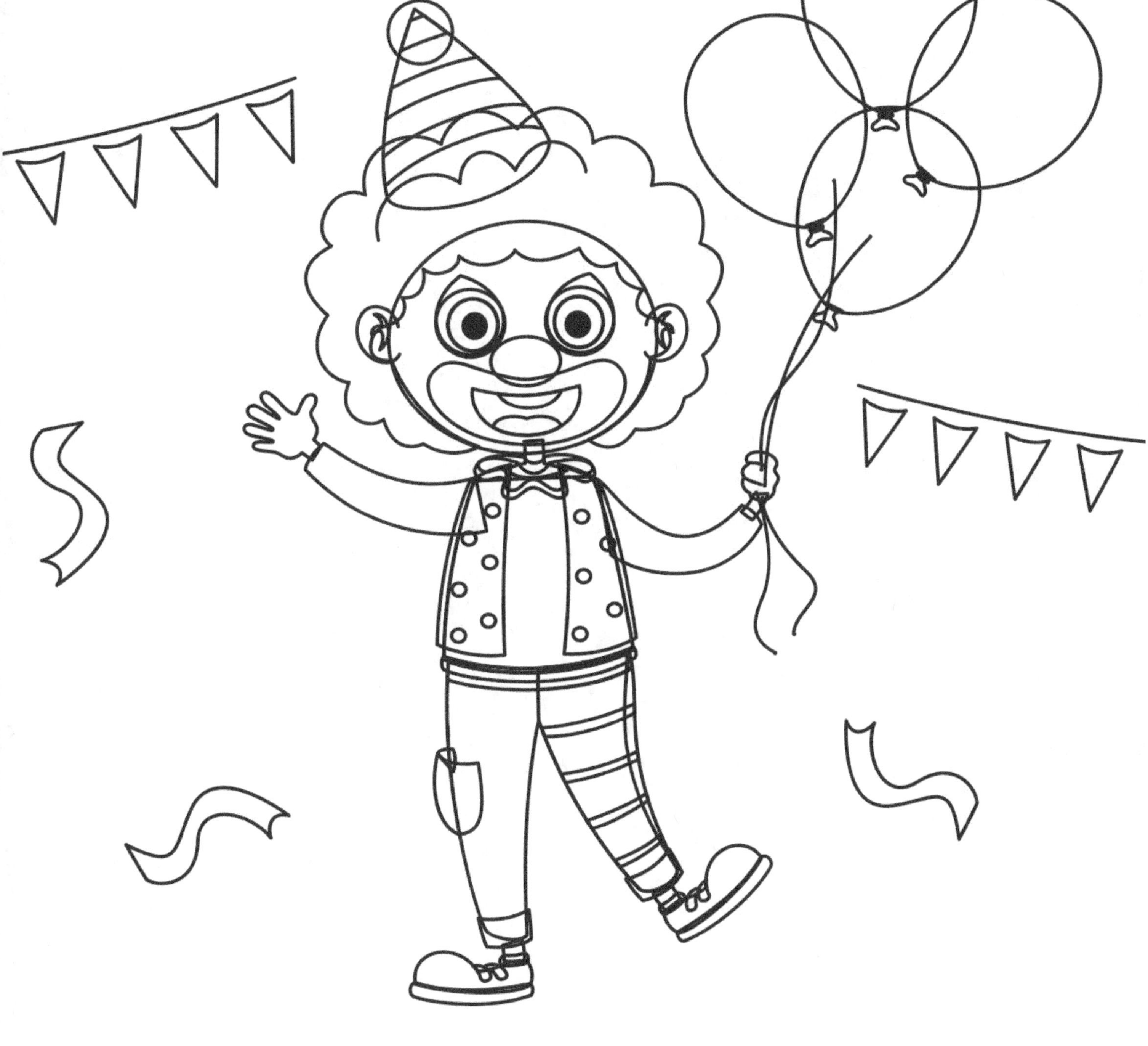

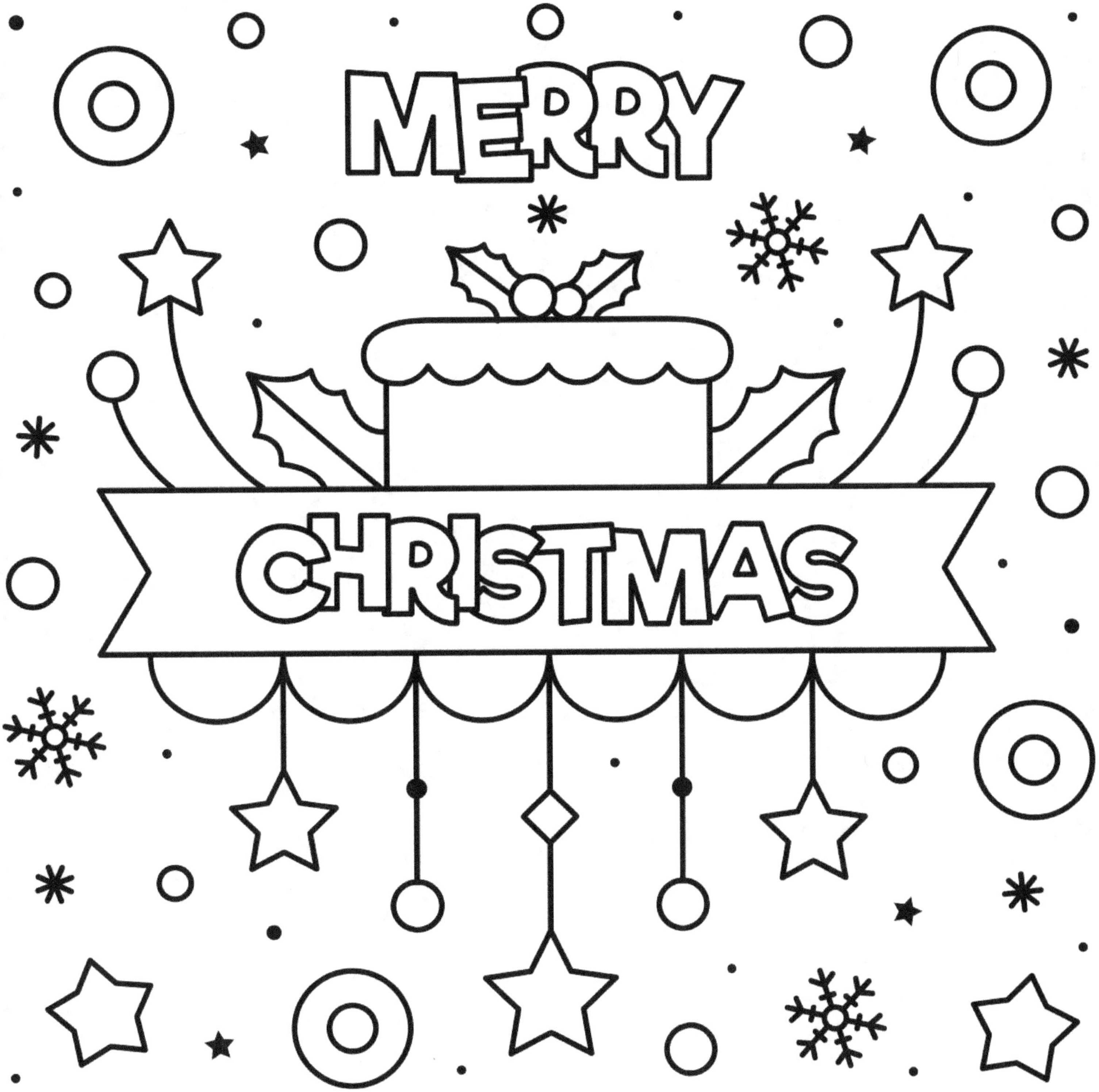
MERRY
CHRISTMAS

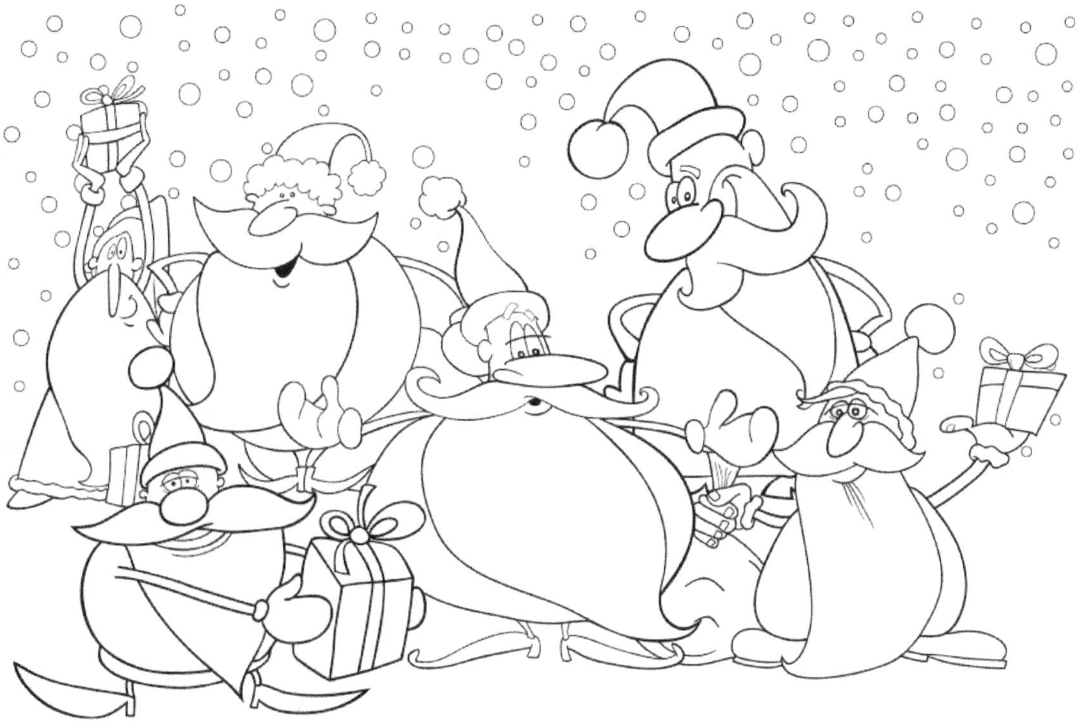

FIND 7 DIFFERENCES

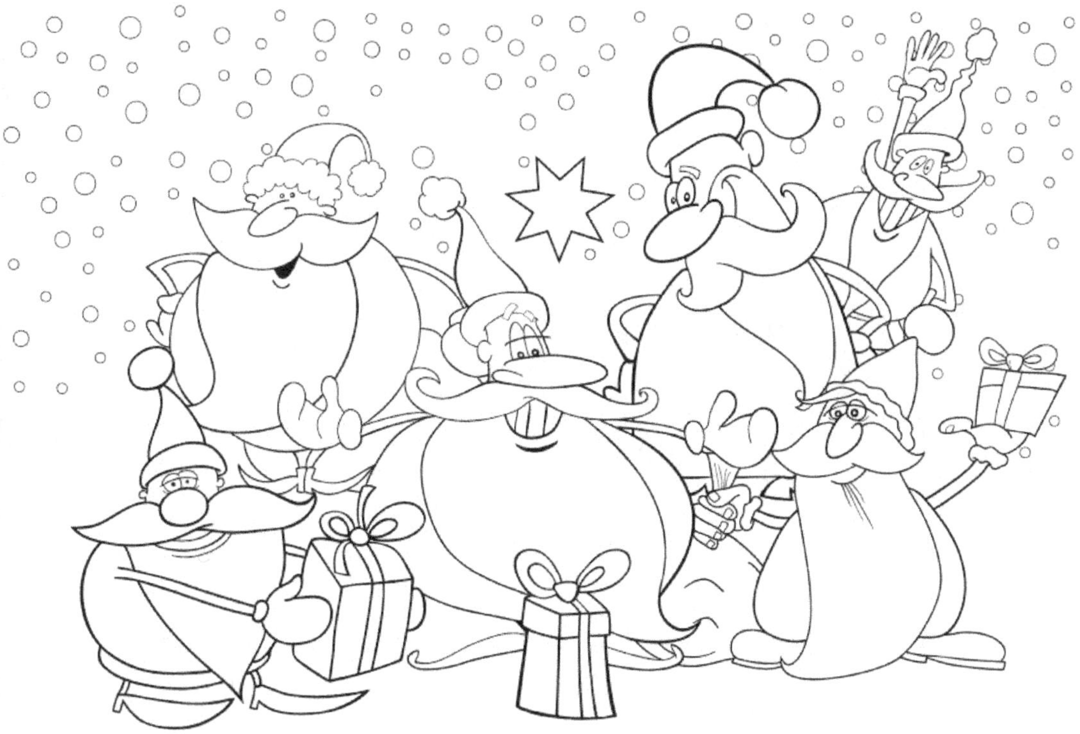

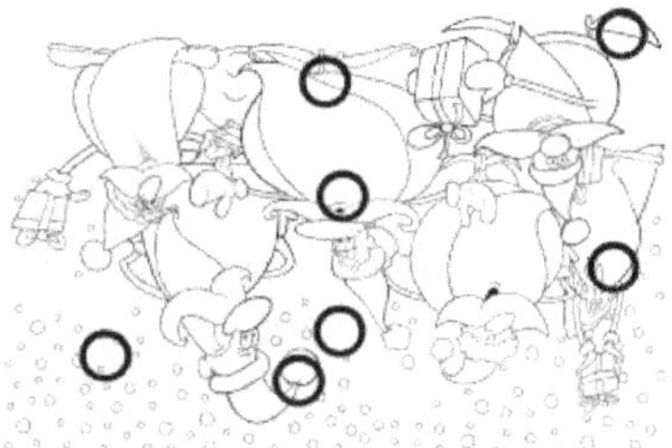

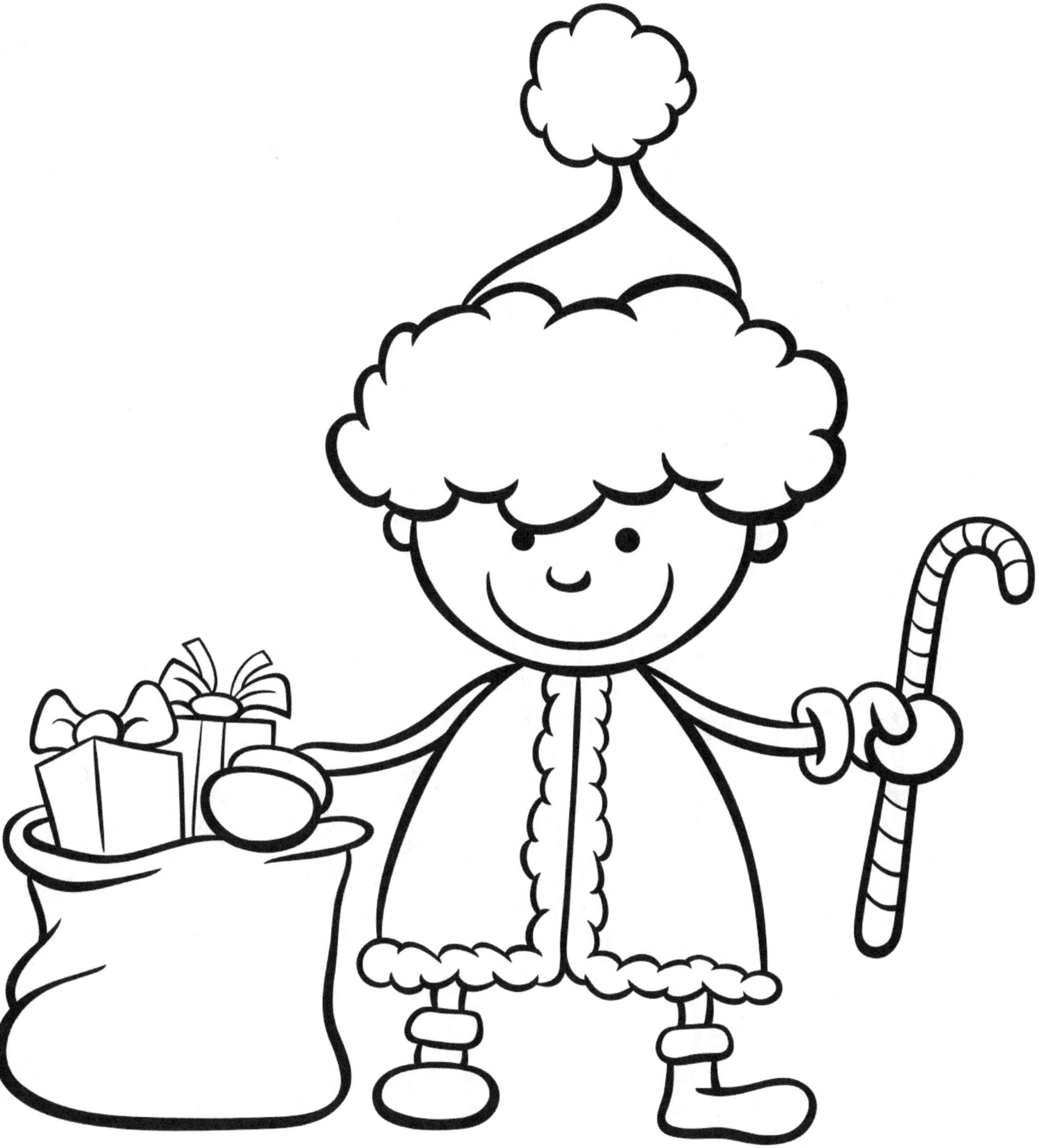

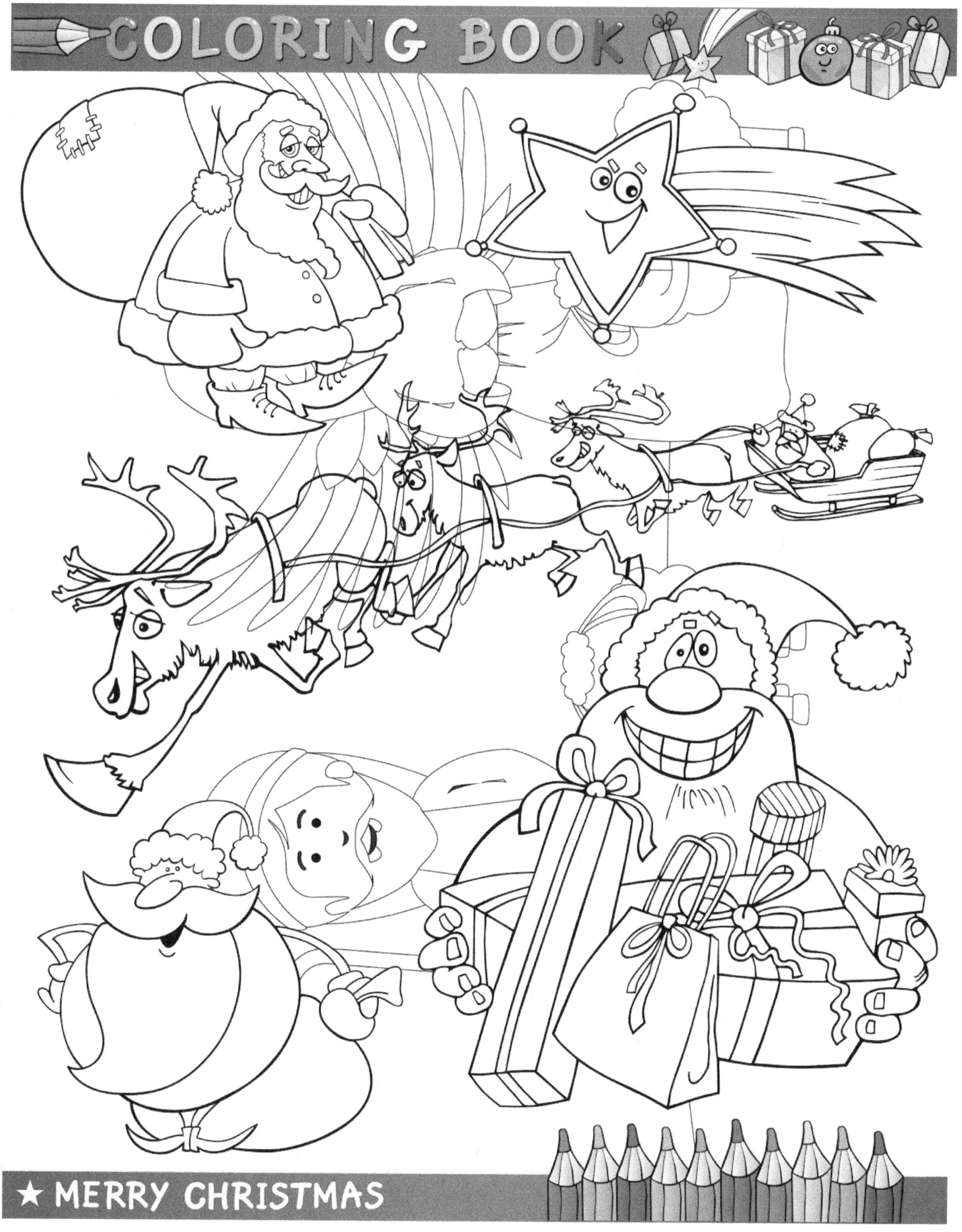
COLORING BOOK
★ MERRY CHRISTMAS

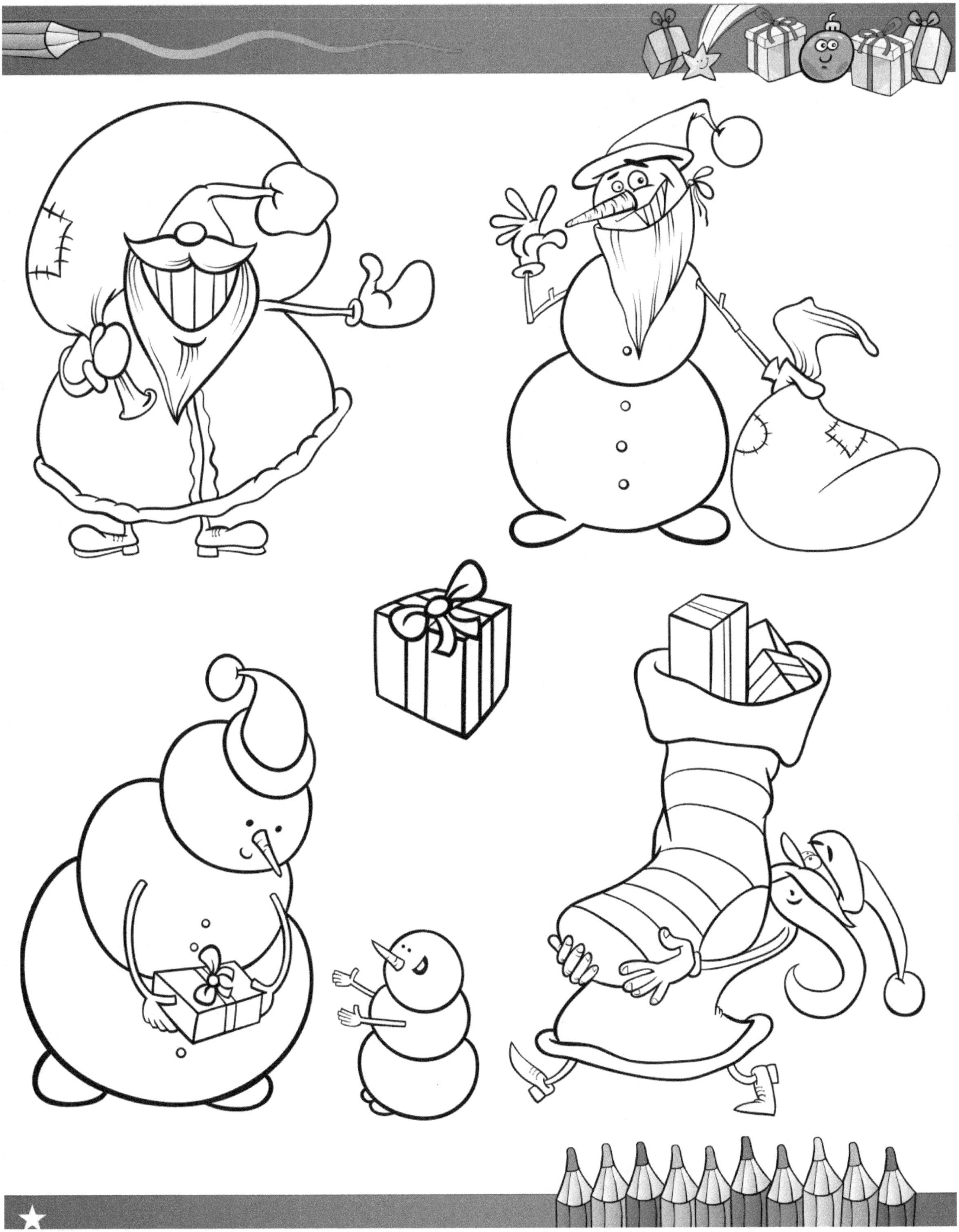

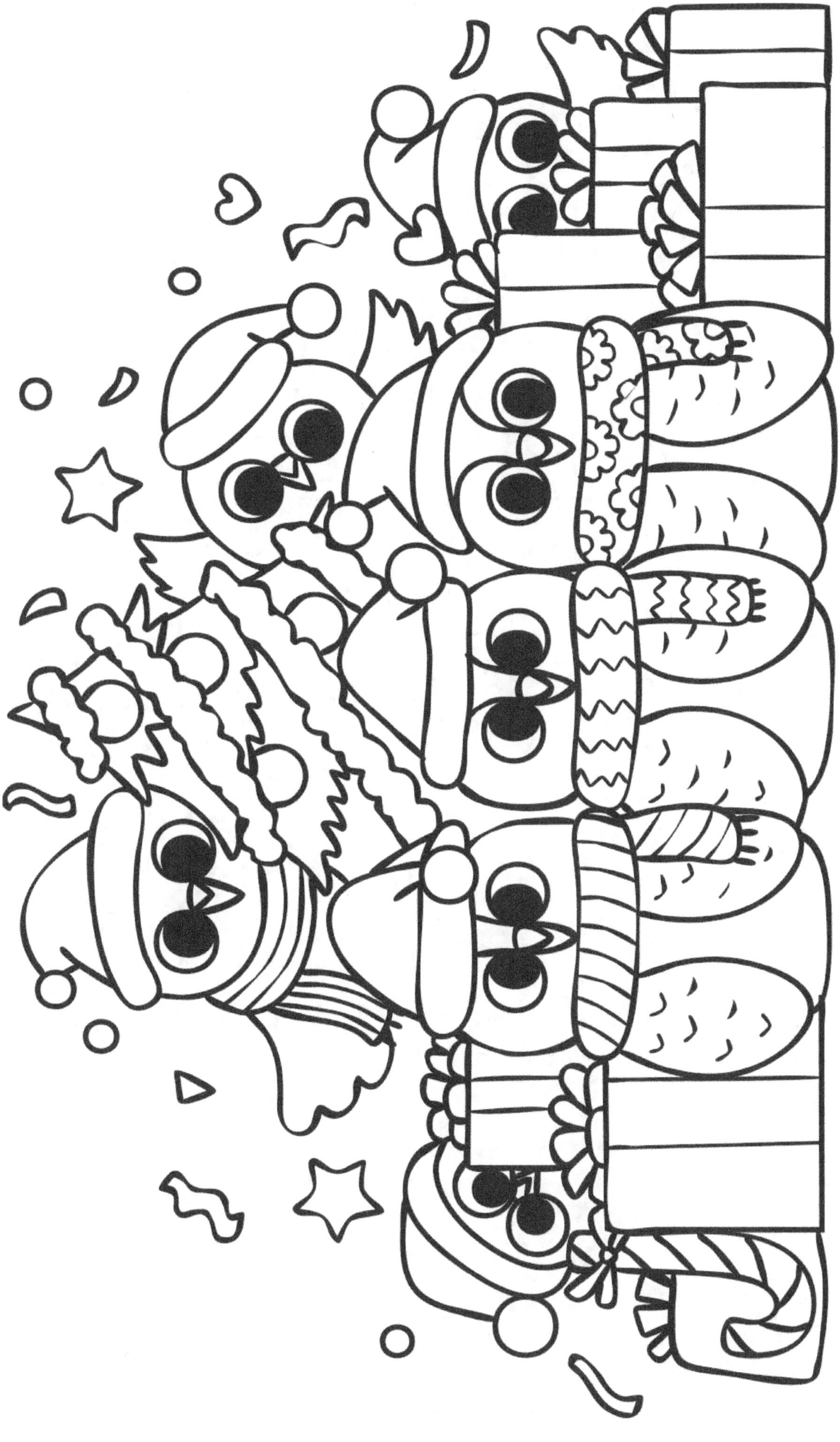

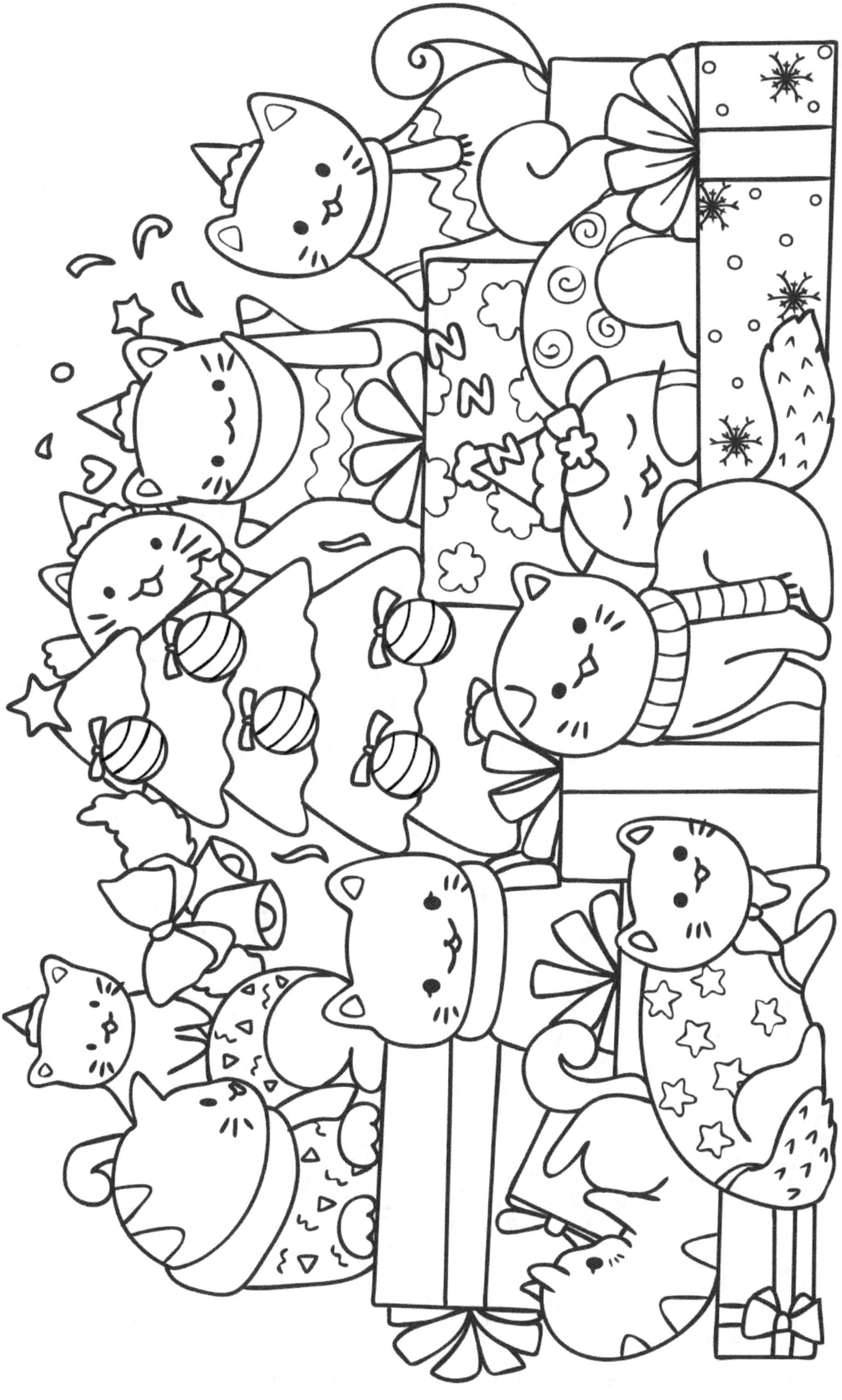
Z Z Z

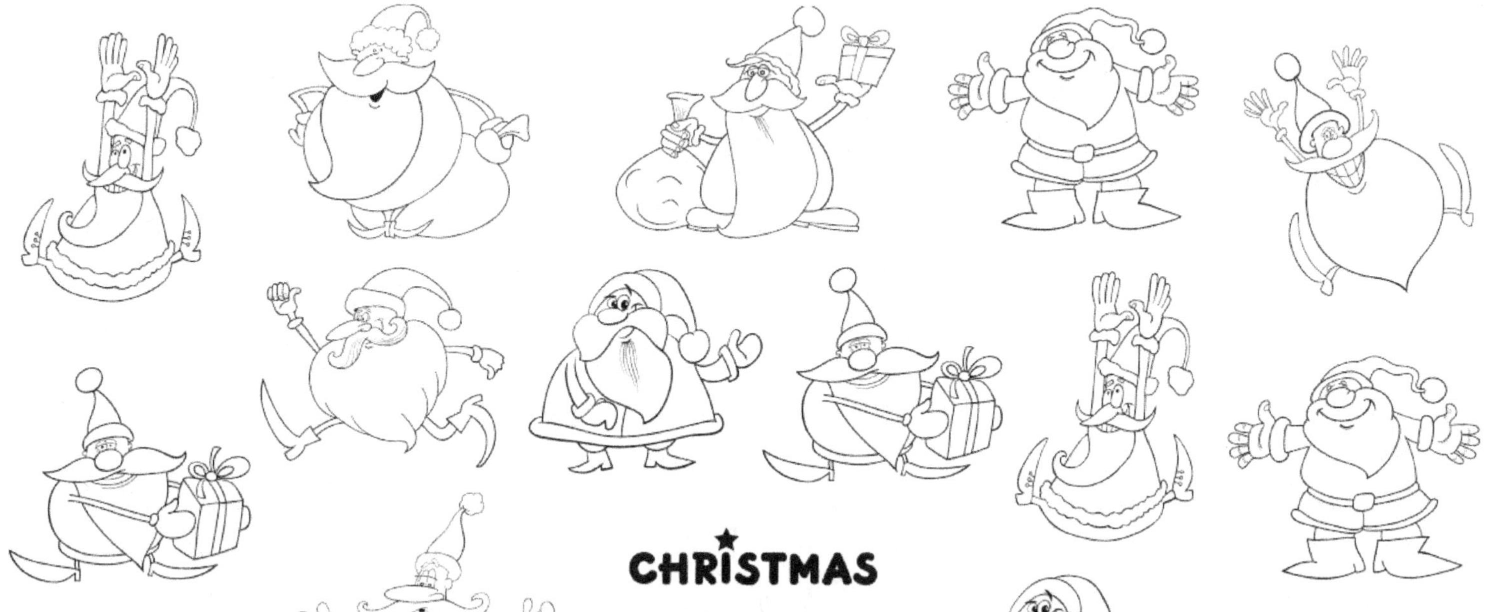
CHRISTMAS
FIND
ONE
OF A KIND
ANSWER

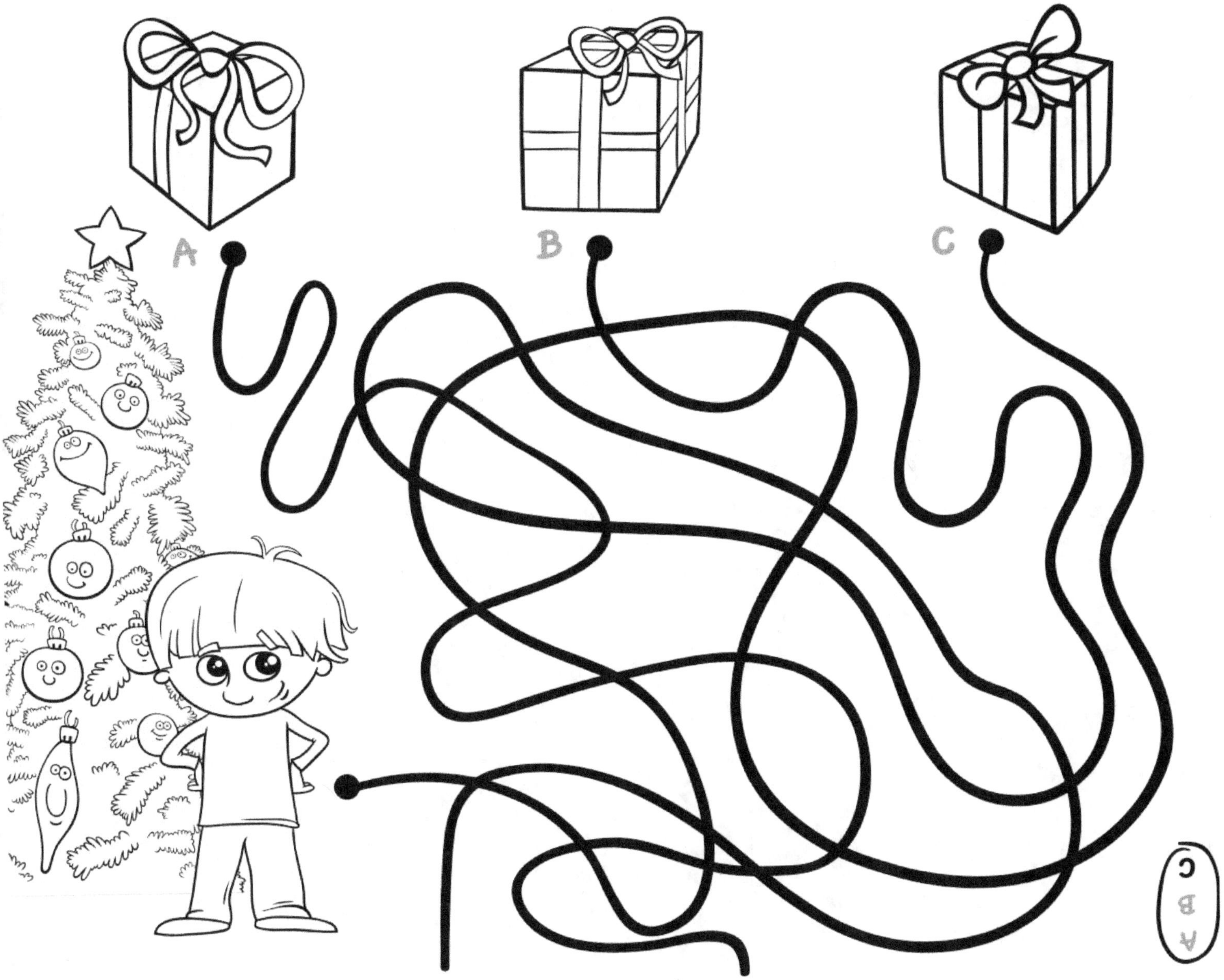
A
B
C

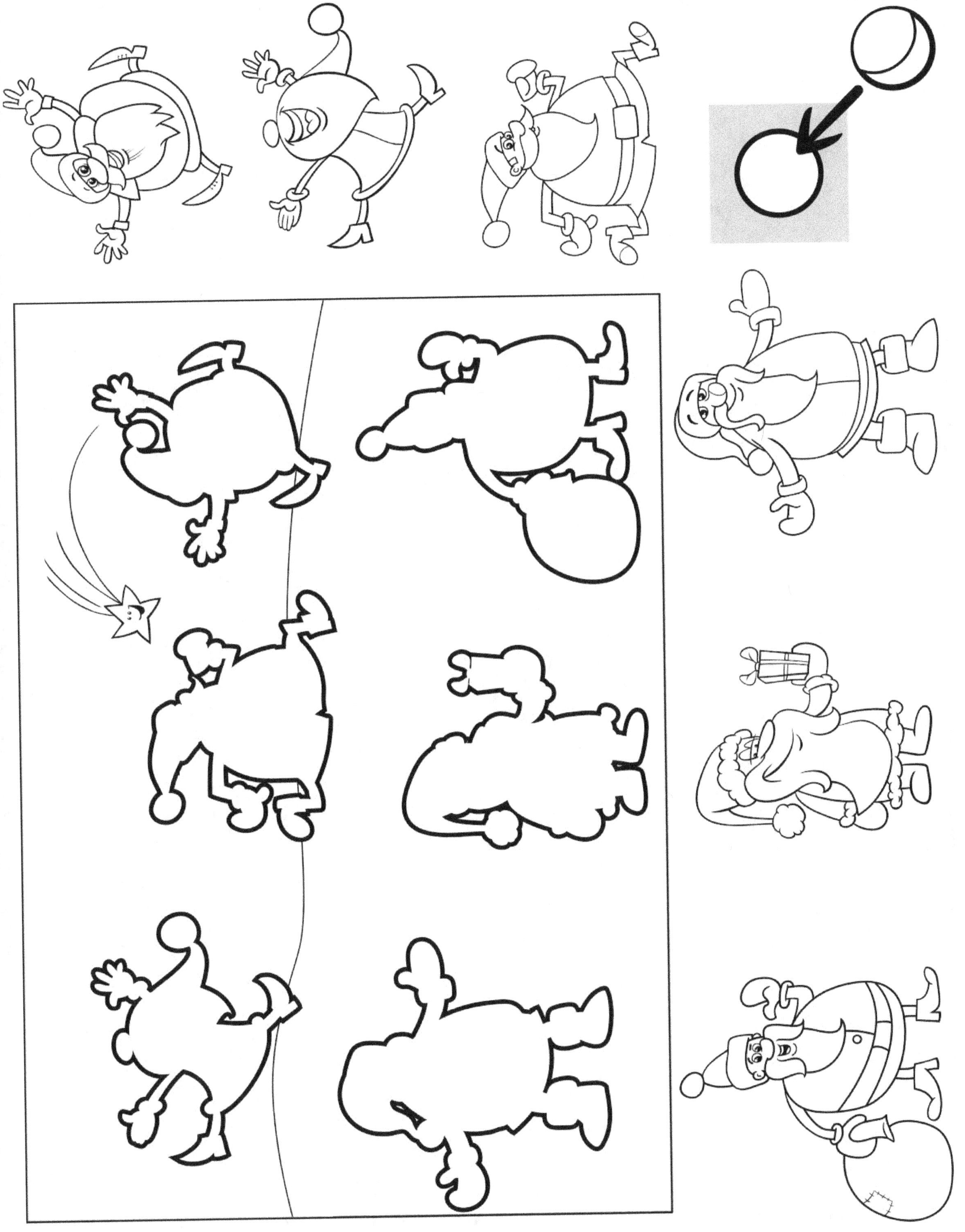

1

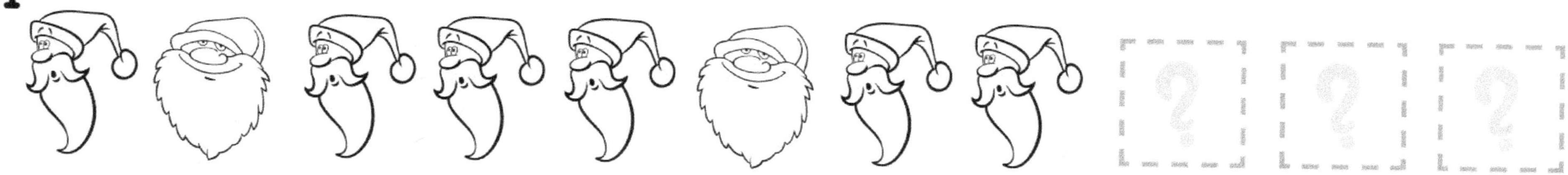

2

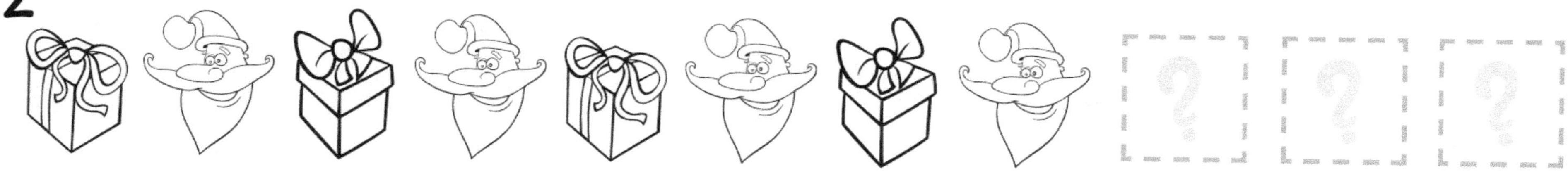

3

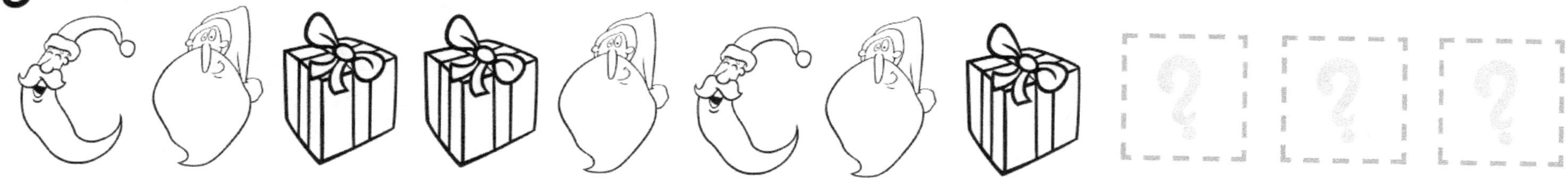

4

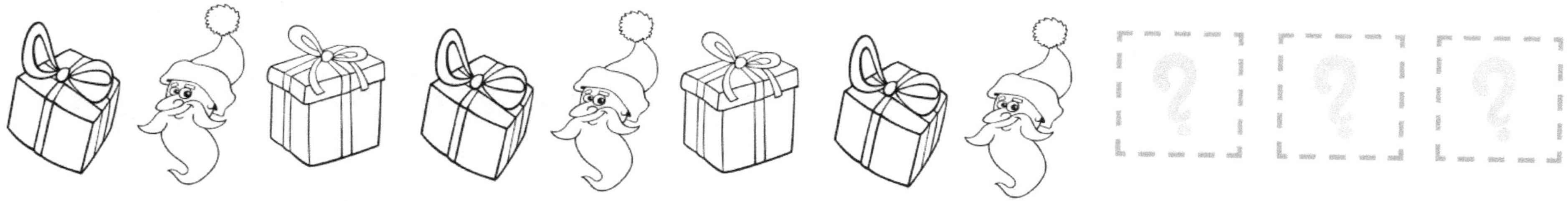

WHAT COMES NEXT?

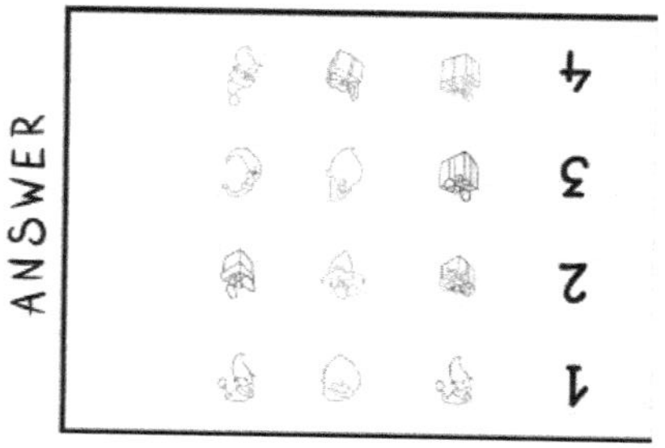

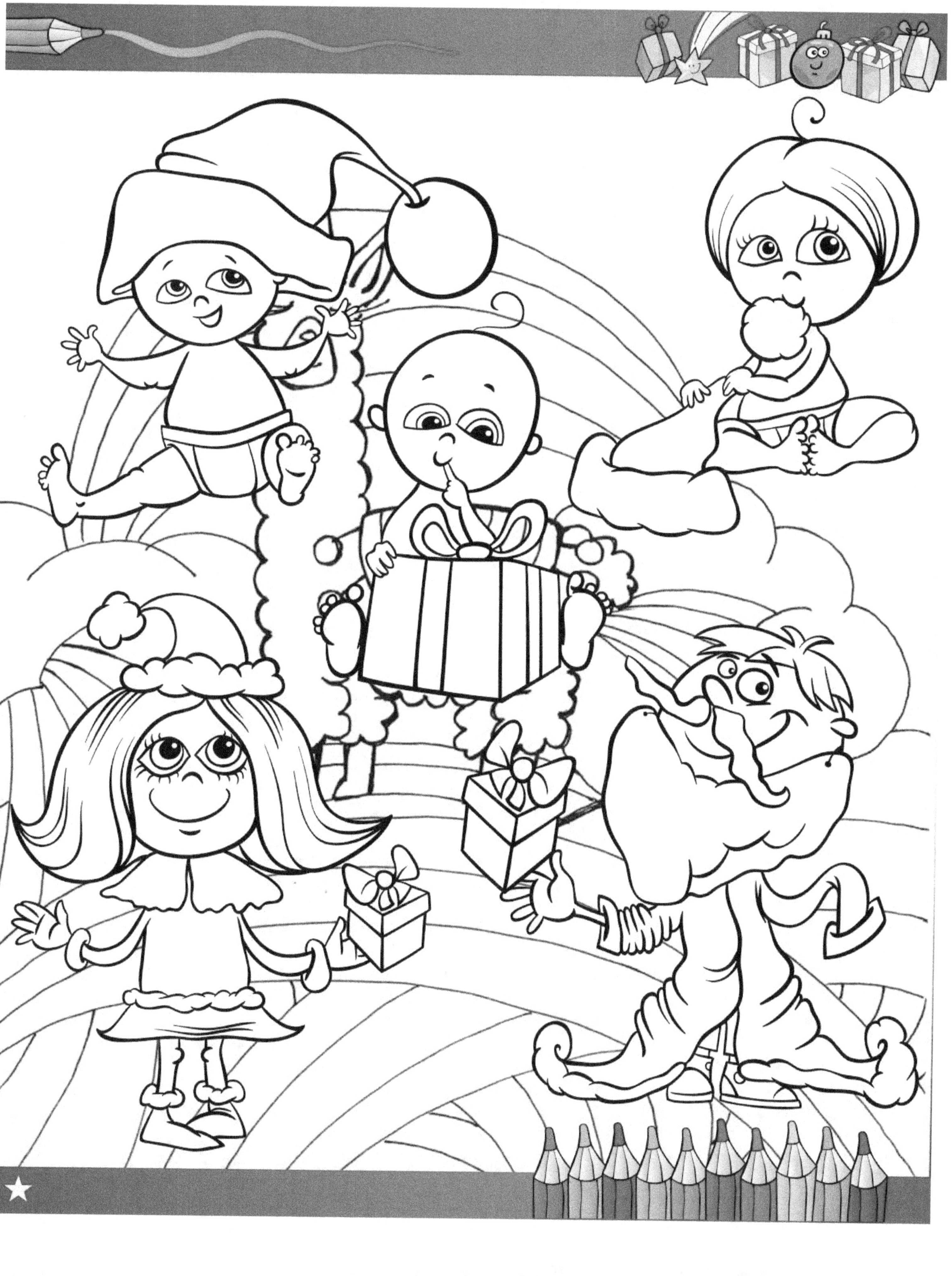

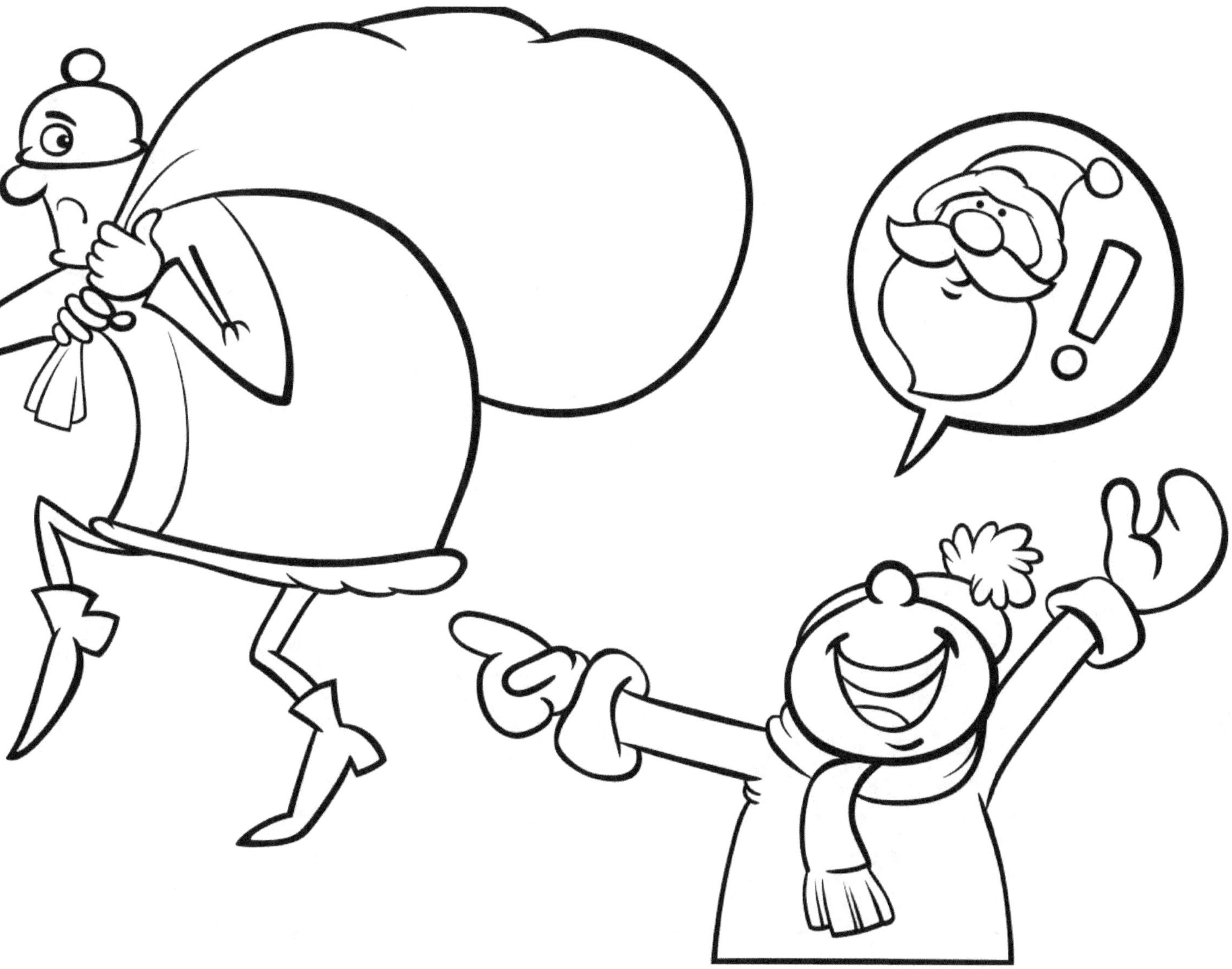

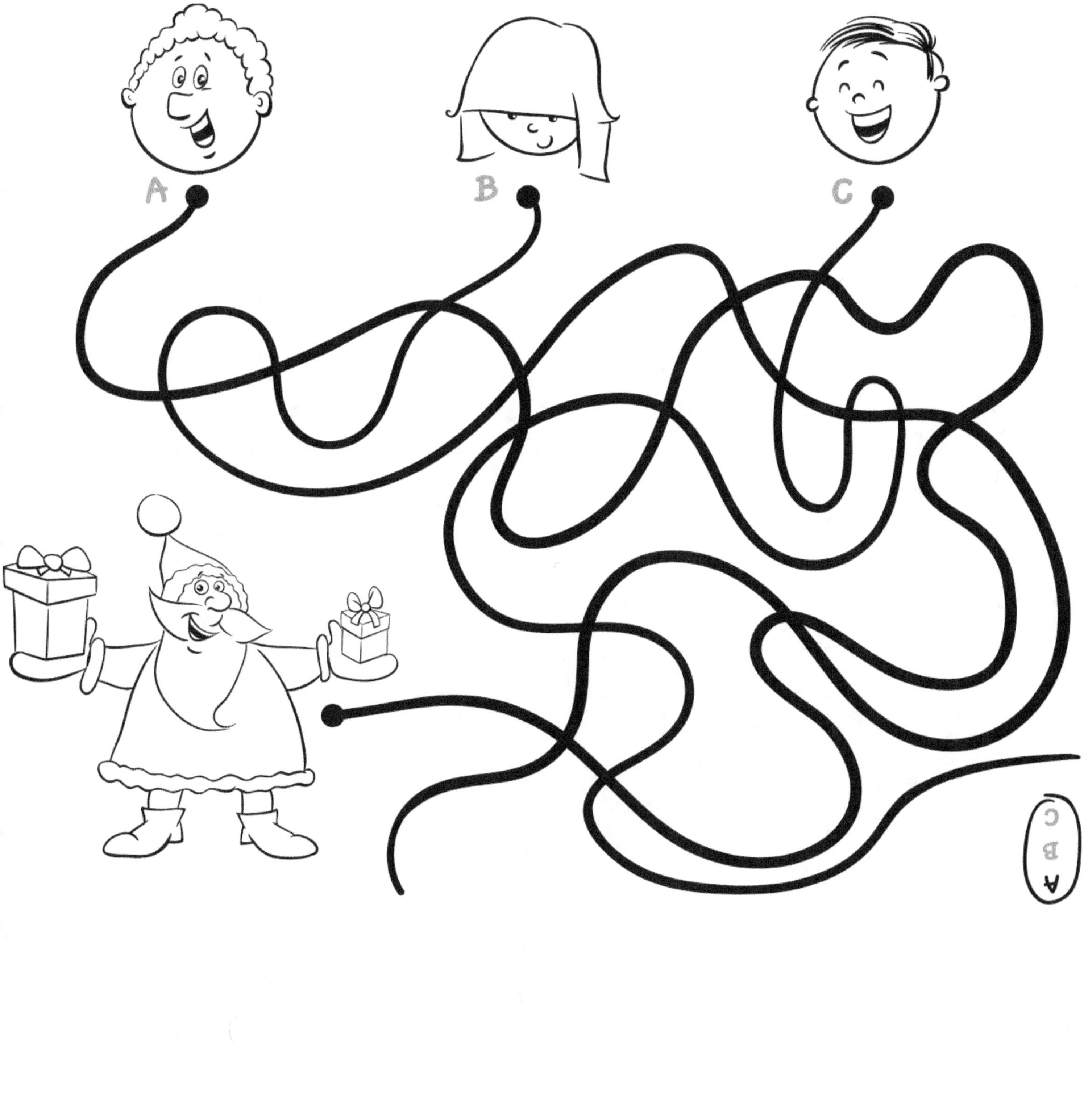
A
B
C

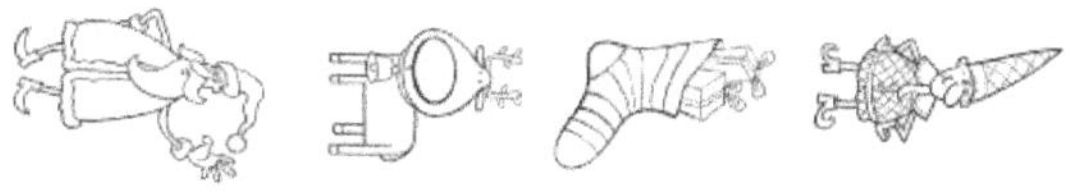

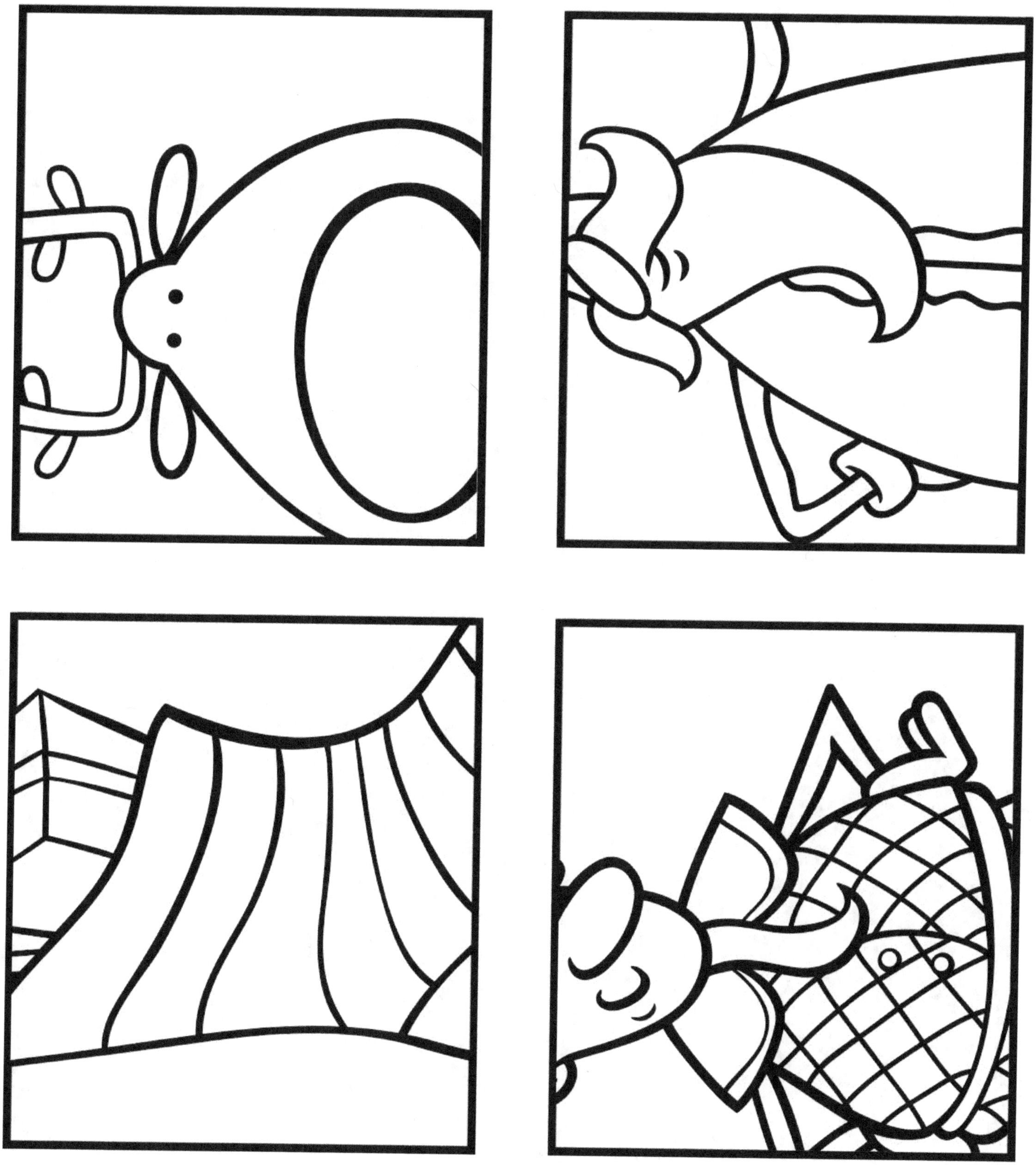

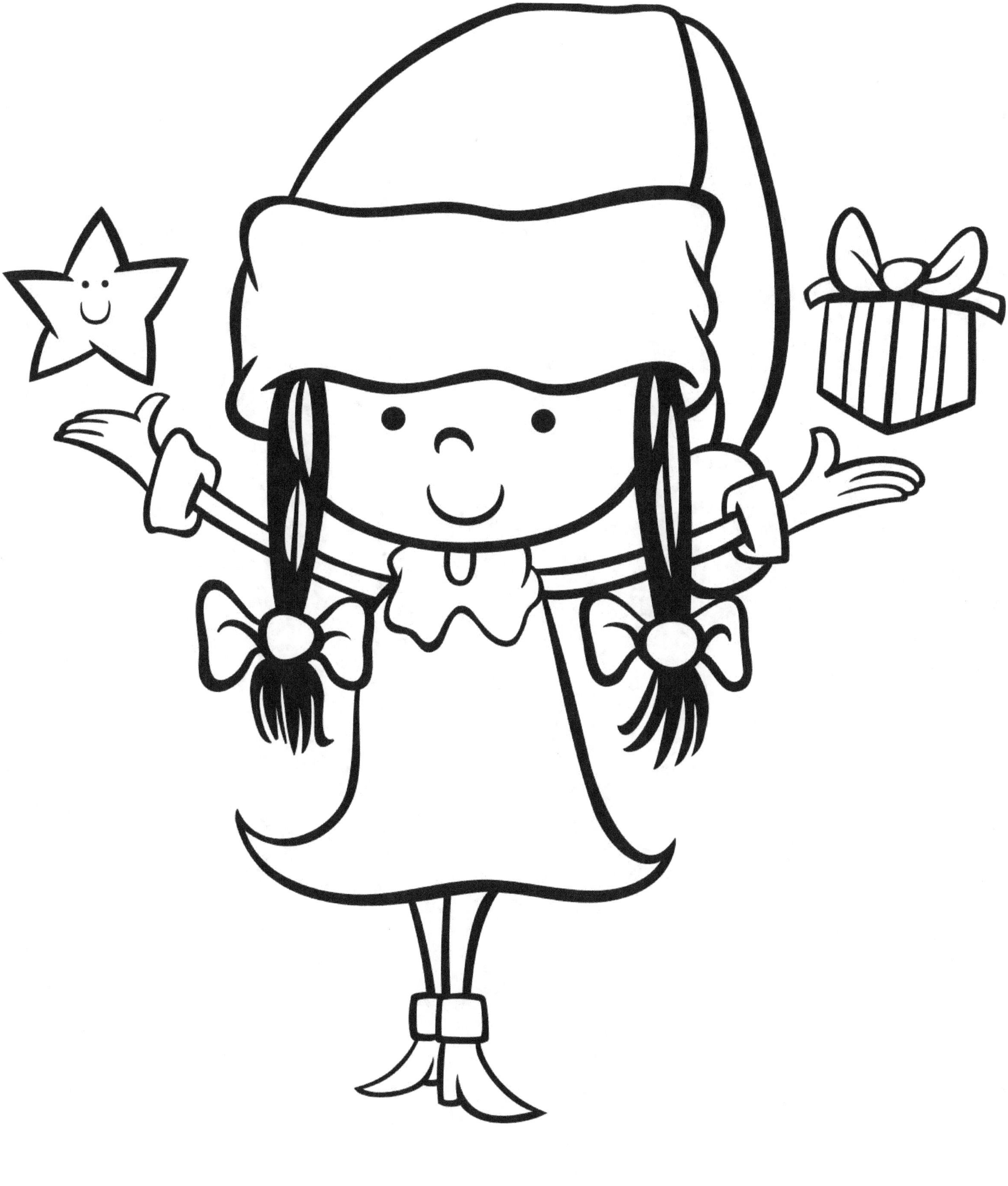

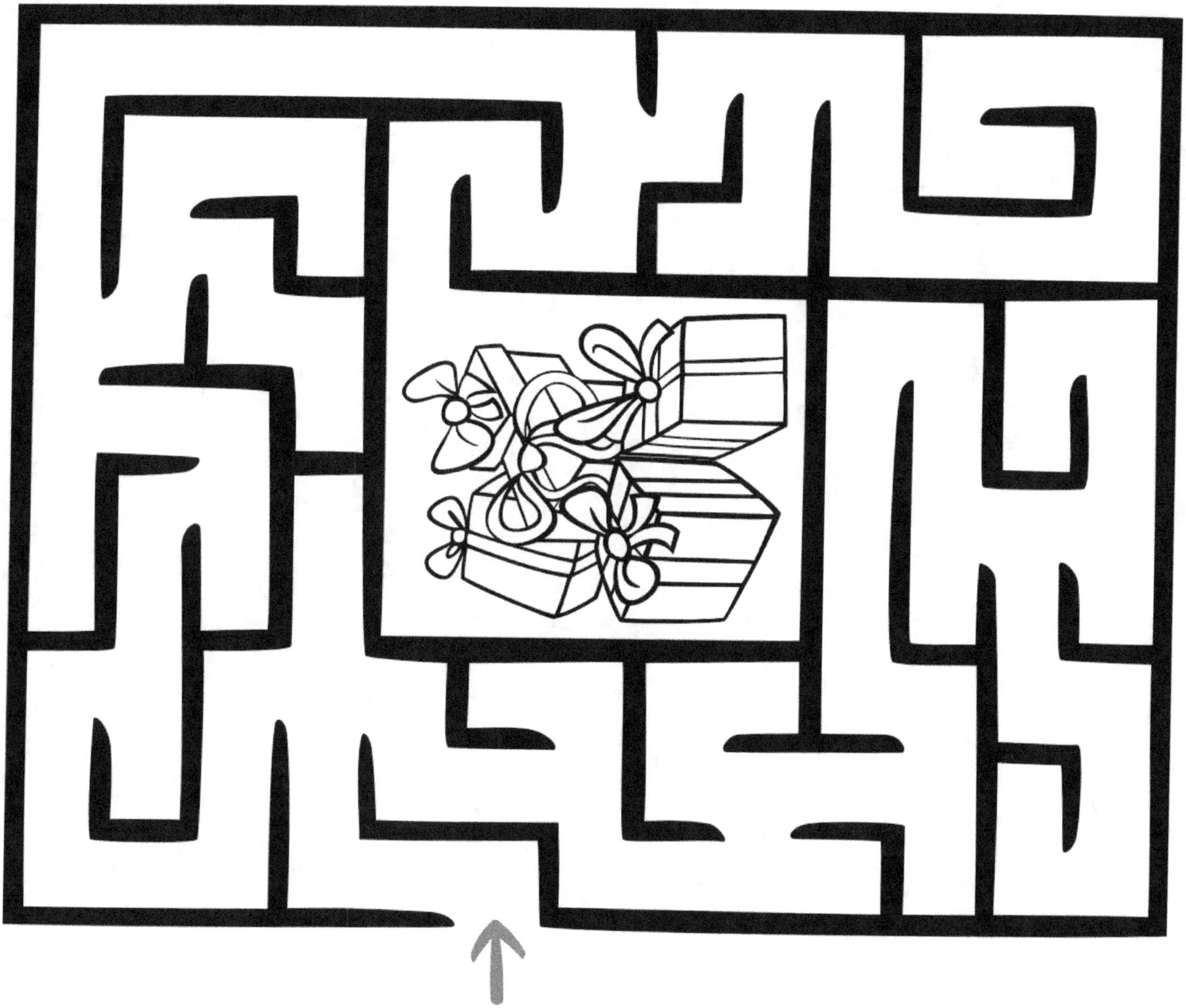

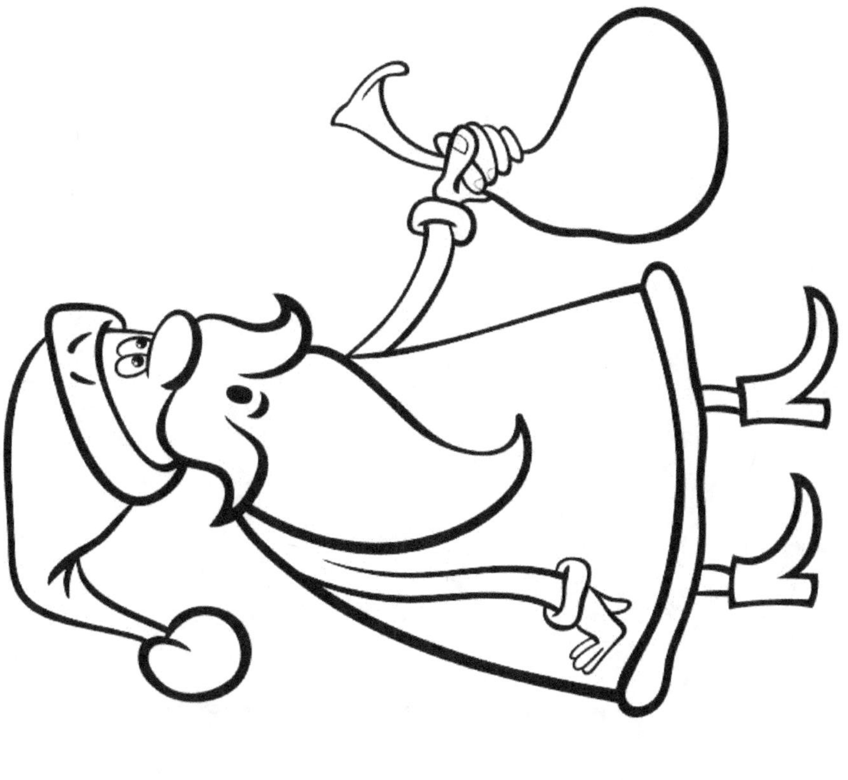

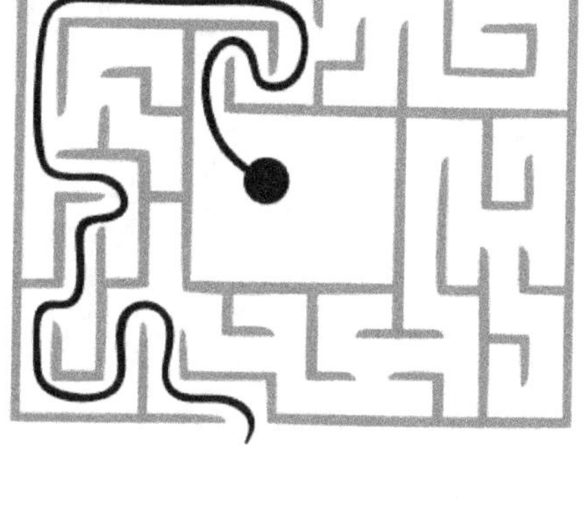

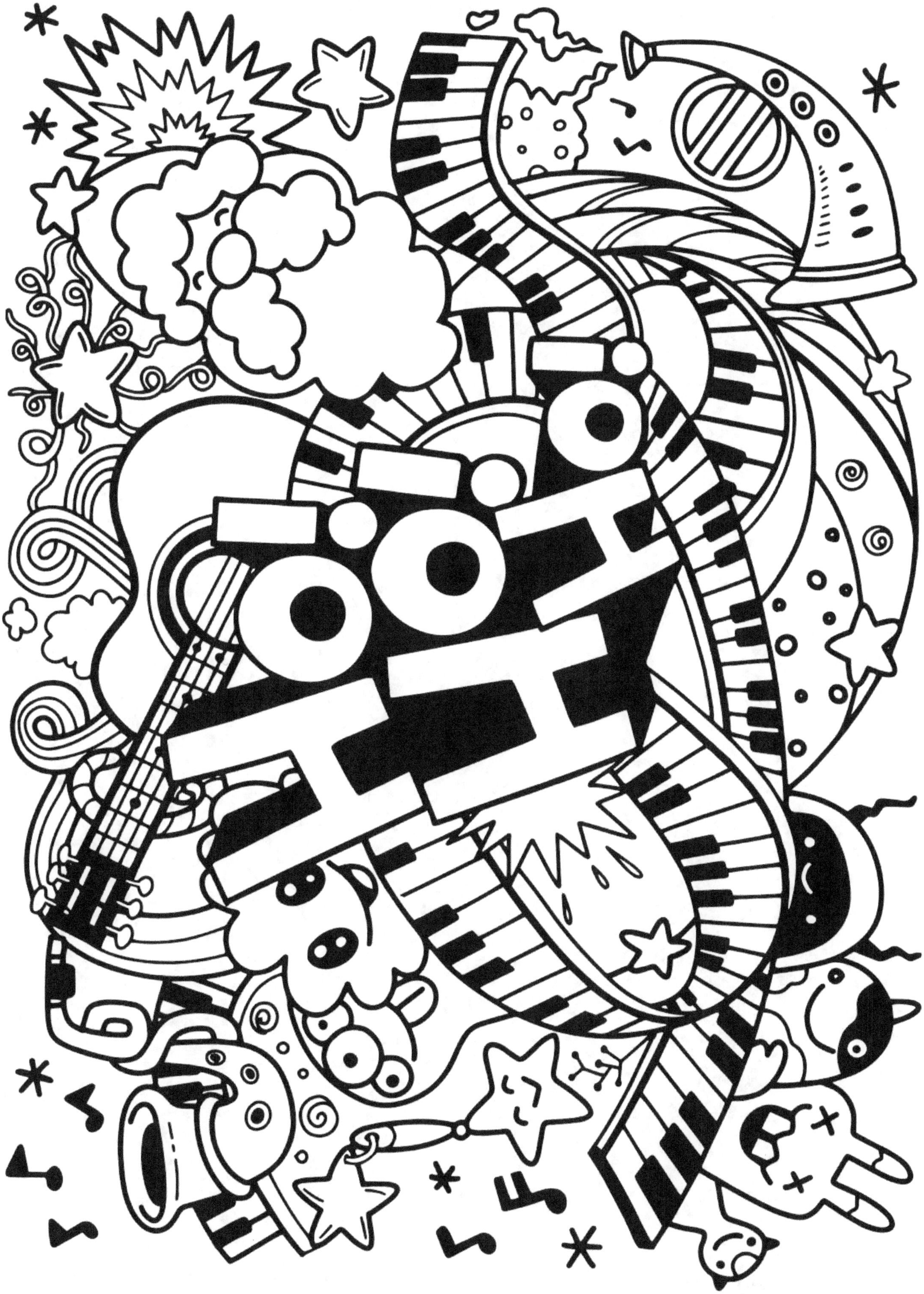

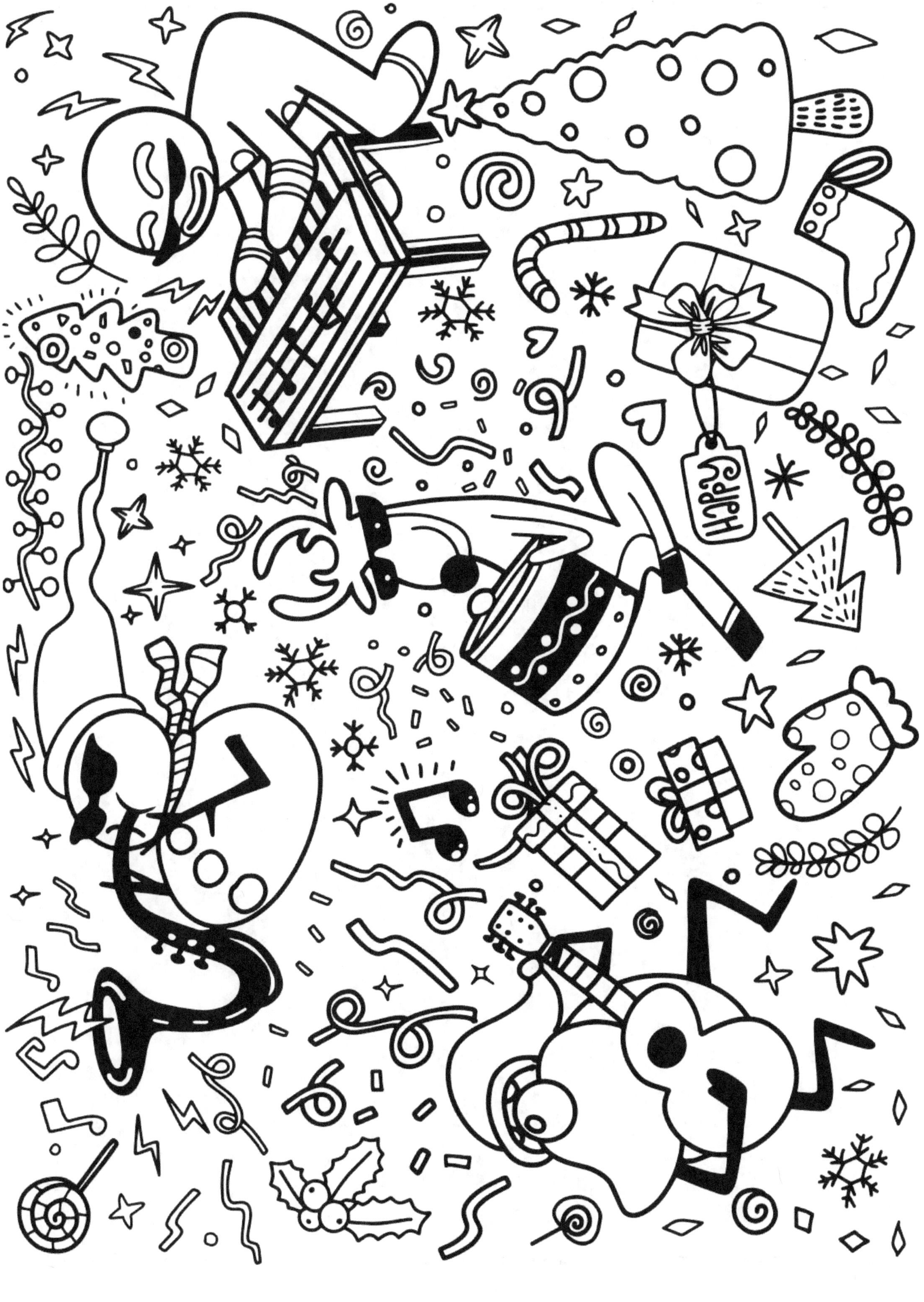
HAPPY

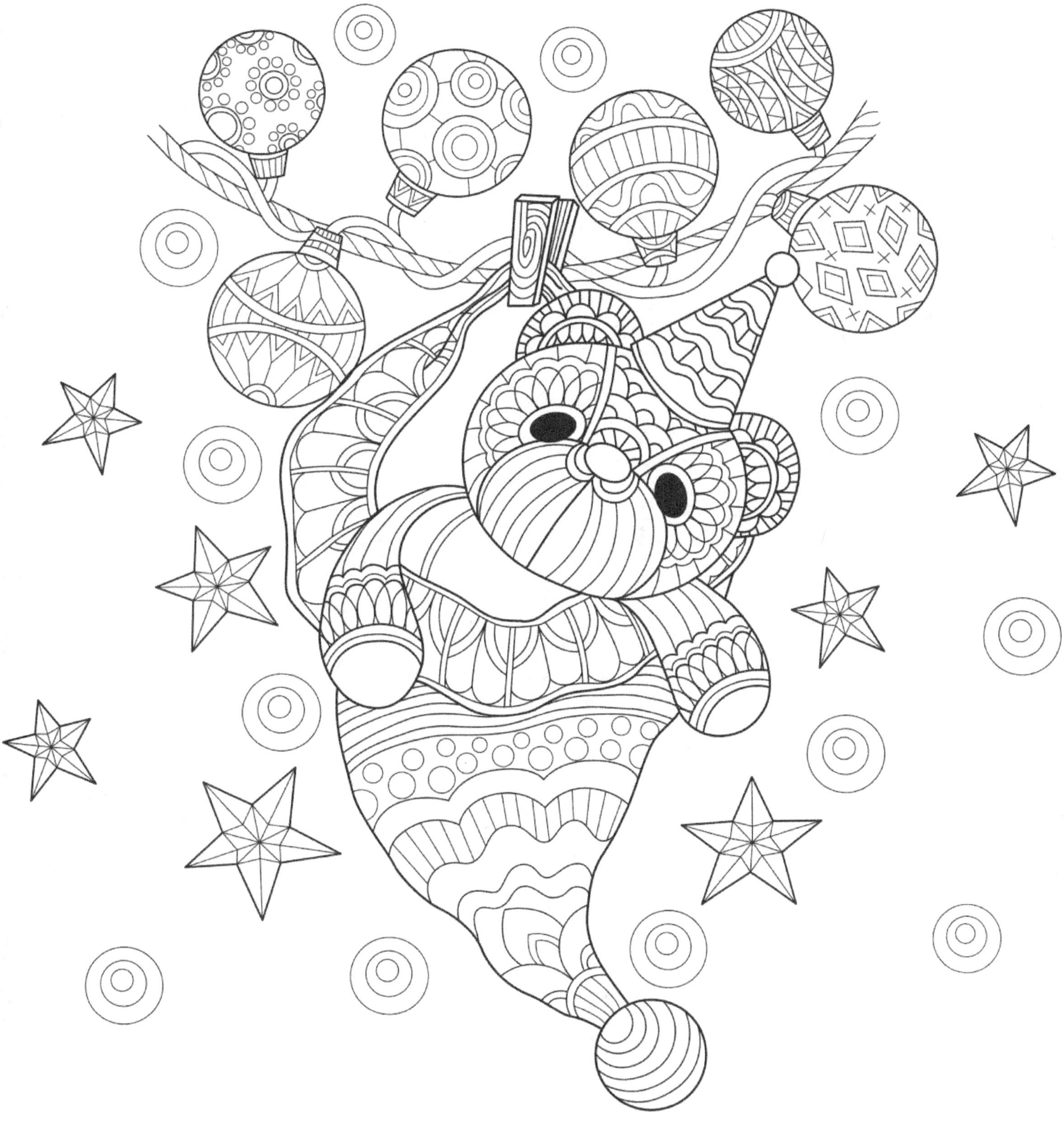

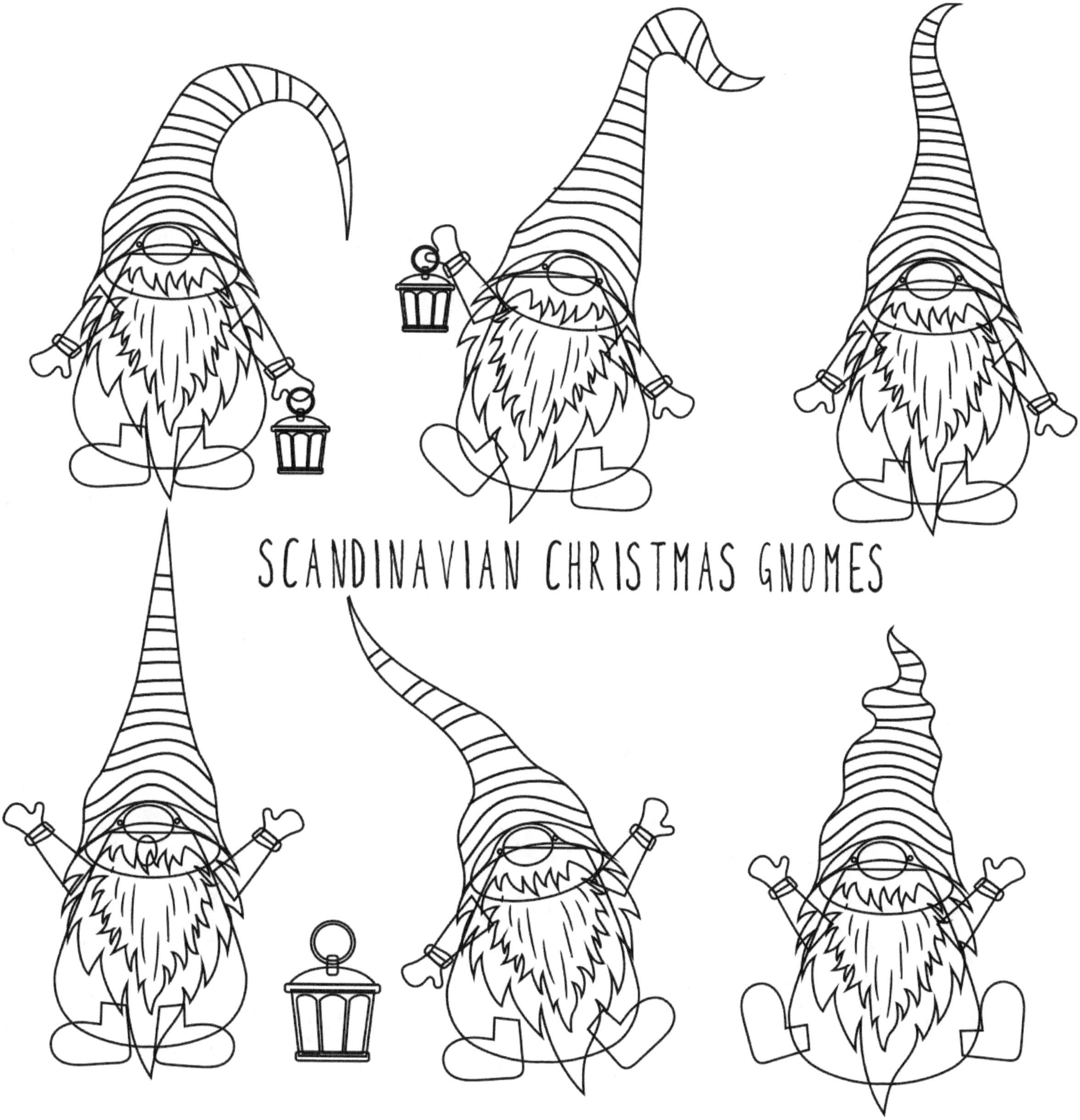
SCANDINAVIAN CHRISTMAS GNOMES

www.ingramcontent.com/pod-product-compliance
Lightning Source LLC
Chambersburg PA
CBHW082154230526
45467CB00044B/3316
* 9 7 8 1 7 0 5 4 7 2 9 9 6 *